Bertha Carr-Harris

Lights and shades of mission work : leaves from a worker's note

book, being reminescences of seven years service at the capital

1885-1892

Bertha Carr-Harris

Lights and shades of mission work : leaves from a worker's note book, being reminescences of seven years service at the capital 1885-1892

ISBN/EAN: 9783743339088

Manufactured in Europe, USA, Canada, Australia, Japa

Cover: Foto ©ninafisch / pixelio.de

Manufactured and distributed by brebook publishing software (www.brebook.com)

Bertha Carr-Harris

Lights and shades of mission work : leaves from a worker's note book, being reminescences of seven years service at the capital 1885-1892

Lights and Shades of Mission Work.

Lights and Shades

—OF—

Mission Work;

—OR—

LEAVES FROM A WORKER'S NOTE BOOK.

~~~~~~~

BEING REMINISCENCES OF SEVEN YEARS SERVICE AT THE CAPITAL.

1885,—1892,

BY

B. H. W.

343341.
16. A. 30.

OTTAWA:
FREE PRESS PRINTING AND PUBLISHING HOUSE,
1892,

CONTENTS.

PREFACE.

~~~~~~~

To write the story of the past seven years of service for the Master as it ought to be written is a task beyond the ability of the author. All that is offered therefore is a series of rapid sketches portraying the main features of the work rather than giving a connected historic narrative. That, written as it has been, amid the rush and whirl of a busy life, it is not free from blemishes which a careful revision would have removed, will be apparent to the reader.

Such as it is, we send it forth with the earnest prayer that the Master may use it to inspire young Christians to offer themselves to God, to be used just when and where and as He wills in the world's great Mission field.

—B. H. W.

Young Women's Christian Institute,
Ottawa, Oct. 1892.

LIGHTS AND SHADES

OF

MISSION WORK.

~~~~~~~~~~~

THE MASTER'S CALL.

CHAPTER I.

I T was a beautiful evening in August 1885, when a young
girl, just budding into womanhood, stood thoughtfully at a shop window watching the sea of faces which,
like a swelling tide, passed down Sparks street on a
Saturday evening, and then receded only to return. What
a sight ! What a study ! To her it was overwhelming. In
the swelling, surging mass were hundreds of young
women with pale, careworn, unsatisfied faces. What a
blessed release it must have been from the crowded,
ill-ventilated work rooms in which many had toiled
through the long, hot, weary hours of the day.

With all the diversities of character, endowments and
capabilities, both physical and mental,—with thoughts,
imaginations and aspirations all on different planes,—she

saw but two classes, those whose aims and desires never reached beyond their own selfish gratification, and those who, having tasted of the unsatisfying earthly streams were, perhaps unconsciously, thirsting for that water " of which if a man drink he shall never thirst."

An intense desire came into her heart as she hurried home that night to gather them into some room or hall and tell them of One who was becoming day by day so increasingly precious to her and in Whom she had found the consummation of all her soul's deepest longings.

Was it a strange coincidence that on opening the Word that evening she should have read the following ?—"Arise stand upon thy feet : for *I have appeared unto thee for this purpose* to make *thee* a minister and a witness, both of these things which thou hast seen, and of those things in which I will appear unto thee. Delivering thee from the people and from the Gentiles *unto whom now I send thee.* To open their eyes, to turn them from darkness to light and from the power of satan unto God that they might receive forgiveness of sins and inheritance among them which are sanctified."—(Acts 26.)

Surely it was a call from the Master Himself. But how ready was unbelief to cry out, " Behold I am a child, I cannot speak," and to apologize for unfitness and to bring all kinds of difficulties, excuses and objections to Him. Again He spoke through His own Word, "Say not I am a child, for thou shalt go to all that I shall send thee and whatsoever I command thou shalt speak. Be not afraid of their faces for I am with thee to deliver thee saith the Lord."

Was it a dream? Was it a vision? Could it be possible that He whom the Heaven of Heavens cannot contain had condescended to speak face to face, "as friend speaketh with friend," with one so unworthy, and that He had really chosen such an instrument to be used in the highest, the noblest, the grandest work in which mortal man can engage—the work of winning souls! Such were the thoughts that forced themselves upon her as she timidly went forth to do the Master's bidding.

The bright, comfortably furnished rooms of the W. C. T. U. were then secured for an hour on Sunday afternoons and hundreds of invitations to a Gospel meeting to be held at 4:30 were carefully written in plain, bold, round hand, but how to distribute them became a perplexing question. A prominent dry goods merchant suggested visiting the work rooms and kindly offered to give an introduction to his employees. It was a grand opportunity, but imagine the embarrassment of a shy, shrinking, sensitive girl, on being suddenly ushered into an immense room where nearly one hundred young women were at work and introduced as "a young lady who was about to formulate some plan for an association of young women, and who will now address you." What could she have said? "Unaccustomed as I am to public speaking?" Surely it would have been the truth. For a moment she was "covered with shame and confusion of face." Unfortunately there was no reporter present to record that maiden effort, and the "address" must pass into oblivion. It evidently made a marked impression, however, upon the poor girls, for one was heard to remark afterwards, "She's a Salvationist," "She's a Protestant Nun," said another, "She thinks she can get us to join a religious club of old maids, I suppose," and a merry peal of laughter resounded through the room.

A terrible temptation came as she left that place to give it up and to throw away the invitations that cost so much time and effort. However, when the next block was reached and the flourishing establishment of R. & Co. loomed up before her, the words, "Thou shalt go *to all* that I shall send thee—whatsoever I command thee thou shalt speak—be not afraid of their faces for *I am* with thee," came like a message from heaven, and when in fear and trembling the request was made and granted to visit the head dressmaker, an opportunity was given of speaking to the girls personally and soon they made her feel quite at home. One sitting by a machine said, "Girls, I think it would be just lovely, let's go."

Inspired with a new hope from this visit, all the leading houses and printing offices were then visited and invitations distributed.

At length the long-looked for Sunday arrived and immediately after Sunday School the rooms were opened and seats carefully arranged, while she wondered if her audience would consist of eighty or one hundred. Surely, she thought, there would not be less than forty, for hundreds of invitations had been given out. After looking nervously over some carefully prepared notes on the text, "The Lord is my Portion," she waited for the first sound of footsteps in the long corridor, but the only sound that broke the awful stillness was the ticking of a large clock which soon caused considerable uneasiness by striking five, half an hour after the appointed time of meeting and no one had appeared. What could it mean? Surely there could be no mistake about the call. It seemed so clear and definite. Almost overcome with the nervous strain of the previous few days, she threw herself at His feet and poured forth her grief and disappointment.

The following Sunday found the rooms again opened. No special effort had been made during the week, but simply to lay the matter before Him and with no will but His she again waited to be used or laid aside. Again the meeting consisted of two, the Master and His willing servant, and a blessed meeting it was. She seemed to get a vision of Abraham who was called to do what his whole soul rebelled against and how, obedient to God's Word, the wood was laid on the altar, and upon it his only well beloved son, that he might be tested as to his willingness to do whatsoever He might say to him and it occurred to her that the Lord might be trying her heart to see whether she was willing and obedient. "He knows my unfitness," she thought, "He could not entrust so important a work to such an instrument," and so disappointment gave way to implicit confidence and with a lighter heart the rooms were again closed.

Another week had passed, it was a dark, wet, chilly Sunday in September. "Surely," she thought, "no one would venture out on such a day," but something seemed to lead her to the rooms once more. Imagine her joy on finding wet foot prints on the stairs, and then seven young women waiting in the upper hall.

The little class of working girls thus formed became eventually the nucleus of a great work.

The attendance steadily increased until scores of girls went each Sunday to hear the "Girl Evangelist." They came from all kinds of motives, some to scoff and to laugh at the mistakes which the Lord permitted her to make in order to keep her humble; others because they enjoyed the bright, cheerful songs of redeeming love; some, friendless and discouraged, came to find a way out of all their darkness into the sunshine of life again. The hearts of these dear girls were soon reached by sympathy and love, and life upon life without a purpose, received almost unconsciously a new impetus which led to resolutions to turn over new leaves, until many had undertaken the hopeless task of their own reformation.

Strange that one so blind had been chosen of God "To open the eyes of the blind, to turn them from darkness to light," yet so it was, until in His infinite mercy He taught through a little incident the much needed lesson of justification by faith.

At the close of one of the meetings a young woman was found under deep conviction of sin. There had been an unusual manifestation of the presence and power of the Holy Spirit as our young worker spoke of the heart

searching question which God put to the first sinner—
"Where art thou?" And He had evidently whispered
to this poor soul, the sad word "*Lost.*" For weeks she
had striven to do the best she could and at last the truth
of her lost and helpless condition was being fully realized.
Never shall we forget the heart-rending words so broken
with sobs—"Oh, *what* shall I do? What *shall* I do?
What more *can* I do?"

"Suppose, dear girl, you give up trying and begin trusting. It says somewhere—'*Believe* on the Lord Jesus
Christ and thou shalt be saved.'"

"But I *do* believe, I always *did* believe."

"Perhaps you do not believe in the right way; what you
want is *saving* faith."

"Well, how can I get saving faith?"

"Ask God to give it to you."

"How shall I know that the faith He gives is *saving*
faith?"

"I think you will feel very much happier."

A new hope came into the poor broken spirit as they
knelt together to pray for "the right kind of faith," and as
they separated she went on her way wondering if she "felt
any happier," while our young worker rejoiced in the vain
thought that she had helped to lead a sinner to Jesus.

Oh, the unutterable joy of that hour, as she looked up into the starry heavens and thought of the angels about the throne, she would not have changed places with one of them. They could not win souls, they could not "preach the gospel to the poor, nor heal the broken-hearted." Once she used to sing :

> " I want to be an angel
> And with the angels stand."

Now she could thank God that she was still in the flesh, and had the unspeakable privilege of labouring together with Him for the salvation of the lost.

Not many days had passed, however, when her *convert* returned looking the picture of misery. She had not yet received the 'the right kind of faith,' poor girl, nor did she ' feel any happier.'

What was to be done? The cry went up from the depths of her heart—" Lord, save her; if I could carry her into the kingdom I would, but I can do nothing—oh do a thorough work in her soul for Jesus' sake." Suddenly the Spirit seemed to bring to remembrance the text : "All we like sheep have gone astray, we have turned every one to his own way, but the Lord hath laid on Him the iniquity of us all."

"You realize that you have gone astray, but did you ever think that the Lord hath laid upon Him all *your* sin and that He had taken the blame of your wanderings? Your salvation is all His work. "He bare our sins in His own body on the tree, that we being dead to sin should live unto righteousness: by whose stripes ye were healed, for ye were as sheep going astray, but are now returned unto the Shepherd of your souls."

"But I have not returned, because I cannot believe in the right way.

"Oh, Mary, Mary, never mind about believing in the right way; after all, it is not so much *how* we believe as *what* we believe. Suppose two men fall from a steamer, both are struggling in the water, when a life preserver and a walking stick are thrown them. The man who grasps the stick begins to sink. Why? Is it that he does not take hold of it in the right way? No, he does not take hold of the right thing. You are struggling in the waves of sin. Your only hope is trust in the finished work of Christ, and it seems a matter of little consequence *how* you trust, believe or grasp it."

"Then why is it, that when I do believe, I do not feel any happier?"

"I am beginning to doubt that feeling has anything to

do with salvation. Our blessed Lord said : He that heareth my word and believeth on Him that sent Me *hath* everlasting life and shall not come into condemnation, but is passed from death into life, whether he *feeleth* it or not."

Soon the dark clouds of difficulty and doubt disappeared, and a ray of heaven's own sunshine came into that troubled face.

"Why, then," she said, triumphantly, " I *have* passed from death into life."

"Yes, dear girl, you have. Let us praise Him for it."

Mary's subsequent life proved that the Lord had done a thorough work, notwithstanding all the hindrances that had been thrown in her way, through the ignorance of one who sought her highest interests.

This little incident marked an important epoch in the history of the class, for hardly a Sunday passed that several did not linger to inquire the way and that dear old room with its green window shades and its newly carpeted floor, became the birthplace of many souls.

CHAPTER II.

A FEW months later found a little band of whole hearted, self denying girls, willing to live and work and die if need be for the salvation of others. But what could they do? Deprived, as many of them had been, of educational advantages, they could not teach; they could not visit the sick and poor, for from Monday morning until Saturday night their time was another's; they could not even give of their slender earnings which in many cases went towards the support of aged mothers and younger brothers and sisters. Notwithstanding, there was an ever increasing desire to show forth their love and gratitude to Him who had done so much for them, in some definite Christian service. Their hearts could echo the language of the little hymn,

> "I will not work my soul to save
> That work the Lord hath done,
> But I will work like any slave
> For love of God's dear son."

Soon a way opened in which their services could be

utilized and their latent powers developed. Several good voices were found and it was decided to form them into a choir and to interview the authorities of the jail and hospital with a view to getting permission to hold services of song on Sunday mornings.

How often has a gospel hymn the advantage over a sermon ! The truth of it touches the heart of the hearer unawares when he is not on the defensive against the gospel. Eternity alone will reveal the number of souls who have been led into the Kingdom through the singing of a hymn, the chorus of which, perhaps, has echoed and re-echoed in the heart long after the last strains had died away.

Permission having been granted, after careful preparation and earnest prayer, six young workers went forth in fear and trembling into the woman's corridor of the county jail.

What a strange scene awaited them that morning ! The classification of prisoners in 1886 was not what it is now. Ten young women who had been arrested late Saturday night and were awaiting their trial, were there in "party" dress. White kid slippers and gloves, a profusion of cheap artificial flowers, paint, powder, diamond dust, &c., were noticeable. Some had evidently been the worse of liquor, some had been smoking cigarettes. Crouching in the farthest corner of a cell was a shapeless bundle of humanity, evidently an imbecile who had been picked up in the woods near the city and retained there for four years. Locked in another cell was an insane woman who made the place ring with her wild shrieks. Several others in plain, loose-fitting "duck" wrappers on which were printed the large white letters C.C.P. (County Carleton Prison) were counting the days when they would no longer "languish in durance vile." One was a little girl, an orphan, who was serving a term for larceny. What a school for a pure minded child !

They felt rather disconcerted at first; however, the matron paved the way for them by saying, "Girls, these young ladies have come to sing to you this morning ; come now, bring up the benches, get seated. It is very kind of them to think of you and to try to make Sunday brighter for you." Hymn books were then distributed and several joined in the old familiar hymn, " Tell me the old, old story." The choir then sang—

> " I will sing the wondrous story
>   Of the Christ who died for me,
> How He left His throne in glory
>   For the cross of Calvary."

One, inexperienced in such work, then followed with a few remarks based upon the hymn which had just been sung, but they laughed her to scorn. Tears came thick and fast as she made repeated attempts to regain their interest and attention, but it seemed of no use. At length, turning to the motherless child who had been the cause of much of the trouble, she said :

"Annie, suppose I were to read in the *Evening Journal* or *Free Press* that you had been tried and found guilty of murder and were condemned to suffer the utmost penalty of the law, and that on the evening before your execution I were to come down here and say, 'You are not prepared to die and I cannot bear the thought of you going down to eternal perdition a lost soul. Here, slip off your convict's dress, let me put my ulster and cap on you and I will arrange my storm collar up about your face, now you may walk out with all confidence, they will never dream that it is you. I will take your old brown wrapper, sleep in your cell and in the dawn of the morning they will lead me to the gallows and I will be hung in your stead and for your sin.' "

Every ear was strained to catch the words as they fell from her lips, even the insane woman seemed calm for a time.

Suddenly, breaking the stillness, the little incorrigible said thoughtfully :

"You nor nobody else would ever do that for the likes o' me, 'cause nobody care's 'nough."

"Yes, dear child, somebody *does* care. *Jesus* cares and 'He suffered the just for the unjust that He might bring you to God.' 'His own self bare your sins in His own body on the tree.'"

After further conversation and several hymns, the meeting closed with a few words of prayer, and to their surprise they were invited to come again the following Sunday.

A short, brisk walk soon brought them to the Protestant Hospital, where they were kindly received by the matron, Mrs. Gooderson, who ushered them into the men's ward. What a change of scene from the one they had just witnessed ! Instead of the dark, gloomy, dismal corridors with their iron bars and gates, were long, well lighted, well ventilated wards, with plants and flowers and birds. There was an air of sweetness and cleanliness about the place. The nurses with their white caps and aprons gliding in and out amongst the beds must have seemed like ministering angels to the poor fellows who had suffering and sorrow depicted on every line of their wan faces. They sang together, very softly :—

"The great Physician now is near
The sympathizing Jesus."

And as the last strain died away one of their number said timidly, "Yes, dear friends, He *is* near and He says to you as He said to Hagar in the wilderness 'What aileth thee?' While we behold various bodily diseases in those about us, God's all searching eye can see what we cannot see, the diseases of the soul. 'What aileth thee?'

Do you say 'I will not believe what I cannot understand.' That is a case of blindness. The little hymn says:

'The blind rejoiced to hear the cry,
Jesus of Nazareth passeth by.'

There never was a blind man who came to Jesus that He couldn't heal—even those who were born blind received their sight.

Do you say 'I don't feel that I'm such a bad sort of a fellow, I'm as good as the most and better than a great many.' Then you must be a spiritual paralytic if you cannot *feel* that you are a sinner. The same Lord Jesus who healed a paralysed body once, can heal a paralysed soul, if you will only let Him.

No doubt some would say, 'I want to have a jolly good time,' 'I want to get rich,' 'I want to get a good education.' There is a burning thirst, a restlessness which are symptoms of fever. Some seem to have the yellow fever, a craving for gold ; others have brain fever and want to be scientific in their type of mind. He who drew near to the bedside of Peter's wife's mother is drawing near to you this morning and His touch has still its healing power. If he sees a desire for soul health He will undertake your case and......and......and......."

There was a pause, an awful stillness. All thought of what she was going to say had suddenly vanished. The embarrassment of the situation became so apparent that she closed the book and said nervously, " Let us pray." There was another painful silence of a minute or so and then she attempted to lead in the Lord's prayer, but even *that* for the time was forgotten.

The work thus commenced " in weakness and in fear and in much trembling " has been full of incident and fruitful in results.

On one occasion at the close of one of the meetings a worker approached an old sailor from the Isle of Man, who " didn't want anyone to talk religion at him," and so he covered his face in the blankets. It was rather discouraging, but she had a message of life for him that morning, and asked why he had started out on the sea of life without the Captain, without the compass, and without having made any provision for the journey. "You have never gone over the way before, you don't know where the dangerous places are."

" And who does, I'd like to know," he said bluntly, as he drew the blankets down.

"The Lord Jesus Christ," she replied ; " He is the Captain of our salvation, He has been over every knot of the way and He knows where the breakers are, and as surely as you undertake to pilot yourself through life without Him, you will make sad shipwreck of your soul." Nothing more was said, but the following Sunday as she entered the ward, her sailor friend was eagerly awaiting her return, and never shall we forget the joy that lit up that weather-beaten face as he said :

" I've got good news for you, He's goin' to do the steerin' after this."

Several weeks later we heard that, while waiting for a train at the C.A.R. depot, he gathered a little crowd about him and told them the story of his conversion, pulling from his pocket a little Bible, a parting gift from her who had led him to Christ, he said :

" Yes, boys, He's goin' to do the steerin' after this, and here's the compass."

This simple, earnest testimony to those poor fellows resulted in one being led to take Christ as his guide through life.

Another incident occurred recently while the regular weekly meeting was being held in the woman's ward, one of the patients interrupted the speaker by crying out : " Oh my God, my God, I'm lost and I'm dying, what must I do to be saved ?"

Quick as thought she called upon the workers to unite in prayer for that soul, while she went to her bedside and with open Bible pointed out the way of salvation. All her difficulties were met with the Word itself, and soon the light of the glorious gospel shone into that dark soul and she was led to rejoice in the assurance of full salvation. Before the dawn of another Sabbath she had been called to walk through " the valley of the shadow of death," but to her it had no terrors, nor was it a dark valley, for shadows cannot be seen in the dark ; the Light of the world was there—even Jesus.

Another door soon opened in the Orphans Home, in a wing of which were twenty aged widows to whom " the Sabbath was (not) a delight," but rather a long, tedious, lonely day. Loss of sight and hearing had deprived many of the appreciation of the Church services and of reading. At the invitation of the Matron a small staff of workers visited the old ladies in their rooms, and after gaining their confidence invited them to the School Room where a short and novel meeting is conducted every Sunday afternoon. Old fashioned hymns and psalms are sung, some of which they repeat from memory without reference to time or tune, after which prayer is offered and it is not an unusual thing for one or two to remain on their knees, through the singing of the following hymn or until aroused by one of their more fortunate sisters whose sense of hearing is more acute, and who sometimes informs them that the prayer was over long ago.

The reading and exposition of a portion of Scripture is the prominent feature of the meetings, and a beautiful sight it is, to see one to whom the Lord has committed this work, and whose life has been made beautiful through the refining influences of sorrow, sitting in the midst with open Bible, while in a sweet, clear voice, she reads of One who has gone to prepare a place for them.

Old " Bi Bi" who long since has passed her three score and tenth year claps her hands with delight while the tears trickle slowly down her furrowed cheeks. Grandma Reynolds stands with her ear close to the mouth of the speaker, and every now and then pats her gently on the shoulder and says:—"It's a bonnie, bonnie wurd, you'll be shûre and come bawck next Sawbbath."

It is sweet to hear the dear old saint sing with quivering voice in her broad Scotch tongue :—

> We see oor fr'ens await us ower yonner at His gate ;
> Then lat us a' be ready, for ye ken *it's gettin' late* :
> Lat our lamps be brichtly burnin'; lats' raise oor voice and sing,
> For *sune* we'll meet to pairt nae mair, i' the palace o' the King.

This beautiful Home which is a noble testimony to the generosity of the citizens of Ottawa must be to these friendless ones, some of whom had been left alone in their utter helplessness to die, a fitting type of the "Home over there" where all is love and sunshine and joy and where "they shall hunger no more neither thirst any more neither shall the sun light on them nor any heat."

Another fruitful field of service opened in Evangelistic Work amongst children. It was felt that " a moment's work on clay tells more than an hour's work on brick, and work in human hearts should be done before they harden." None are so easily influenced and few so easily won as the little ones. Their simple unquestioning faith enables them to grasp the plan of redemption when many an older one has stumbled over it because of its very simplicity. Strange that so few direct, personal and persistent efforts have been put forth for their immediate conversion in the Church, in the Sunday School and in the home. We cannot be too thankful for the Sunday Schools, which have accomplished a great work among the children, but how many Sunday School teachers have hindered the little ones from coming to Jesus! They teach Bible history and geography, they tell them that if they will try to be good and do the best they can that they will go to heaven when they die, and they wait until they reach what they consider an age of responsibility before they tell them that they are poor, lost, guilty, helpless sinners needing salvation. Is it not true of a child as of a man that except he be born again he cannot see the Kingdom of God?

Dr. Dwight, of Yale College, speaking of the desirability of labouring for the early conversion of children, says:

"The conscience is at this period exceedingly tender and susceptible, readily alarmed by the apprehension of guilt. All the affections also are easily moved and are fit to retain permanently and often indelibly whatever impressions are made. To every good thing the heart is drawn, comparatively without trouble or resistance and united by bonds which no future art or force can dissolve."

It was laid upon their hearts to gather in the little ones and to speak to them of their need of One to save them from the guilt, the penalty, and the power of sin. The various Schools were visited, and an opportunity given of addressing the children in the different class rooms, and inviting them to a meeting in the Coffee House Hall. The novelty of a children's evangelistic meeting drew upwards of 600 to the hall long before the hour intimated, and as the number of workers was quite insufficient to cope with such a crowd, confusion reigned supreme. Repeated attempts were made to gain their interest and attention, but it was of no avail. Suddenly the secretary of the Y. M.C.A. appeared on the scene, and after making his way through the crowd with much difficulty reached the platform and began clapping his hands together in a violent manner. It had the desired effect, for in less than two minutes their undivided attention was given.

" Now," said he, " proceed : "

Holding up a little book our young worker, who was beginning to realize that she had, perhaps, more zeal than judgment, said : " Children I have a strange picture book to show you this afternoon, and though there are no words nor letters printed or written in it there is a wonderful story there, I wonder were I to show you the different pages if you could read it. Look, the first is black, the next red, then white and gold."

The first is a picture of the heart of every boy and girl in this Hall, before they ask the Lord Jesus to wash away there sins. There is nothing in all this earth so black as sin. Once there was a contagious disease that broke out in the old country that they called the black plague ; nearly everybody caught it and there were so many sick people that the Doctors couldn't go and see them all, and hundreds and thousands died and they couldn't get hearses and coffins enough to bury them ; so they dug a big pit, and they sent black carts through streets to collect the bodies which were thrown into the pit. There was black on almost every door, and the people were all in black ; it was one of the saddest pictures in the pages of English history. But there is a blacker plague than that in the world now. It broke out in the garden of Eden, and it spread over the whole earth, there is not a man, a woman or a child who has it not ; I mean *sin*. God says :

"There is no difference, for *all* have sinned and come short of the glory of God," and "sin when it is finished bringeth forth *death*." Ah ! boys and girls it is a *black* picture is it not ? Let us leave it and look at the next :—

RED.—Do you know what that means? That "the blood of Jesus Christ, God's son, cleanseth us from all sin." A little boy was dying one day and the Minister called and said : "Freddy you've been a naughty boy ; are you not afraid to die ?" "No sir," he said, confidently. "Why," said the Minister "will you not be afraid when the Judge of all the earth shall call you before him and show you the big book in which all your naughty words and deeds are written down ?"

"No sir," he replied, "I know I've been naughty and I know it's written down, but when the book is taken out Jesus will draw his pierced hand over it and blot it all out with his own blood so that the Judge can't see."

"How do you know He will, my boy ?"

Because the Golden Text last Sunday said : "I even I am He that blotteth out thy transgressions and will not remember thy sins."

Dear boys and girls, Jesus wants you to trust Him just as Freddy did.   He wants you to come to Him for forgiveness of all your sins ; He says, "Suffer the little children to come unto me,"

A little girl said once : "How can I come to Jesus ? He's a great way up, and I'm a great way down, and I don't know how to come ;" she went to her Papa for help but He could not tell her, nor could her mother, for they had not come themselves. At length, going to her own little room, and kneeling down, she said : "Dear Jesus, I don't know how to come but I just DO come." When we come to Him in this way He will give us hearts pure and white and clean like this," (holding up the white page.)

Let us take David's prayer and make it our own. "Wash me, and I shall be whiter than snow." Then shall we be ready to enter with Him into that city which is of pure gold, and which has no need of the sun neither of the moon to shine in it, for the Glory of God does lighten it and there shall in no wise enter in to it anything that defileth, "but they which are written in the Lamb's book of life."

In this simple way, and by means of object lessons, an effort was made to bring the truths of the Gospel within the comprehension of the little ones and at the same time to retain their interest. The attendance kept up wonderfully during the first year, and until the place of meeting was changed, when there was suddenly a great falling off, and the work has not since been resumed on the same scale.

The experience of that year, however, proved that there are few fields of Christian service in which as rich a harvest of souls may be gleaned for the Master as in

work among children. Testimonies like the following
were received through the mail :—

MY DEER TEECHER,—

i love Jesus Bcause he dide to saave me and i want to
B his littel girl but i'm sow notty that I dont no how.

Your loving frend,

M. A.

DEAR MISS ,—

You will be glad to hear that I have turned a Cristian
and God has forgave all my sins and converted me. Pray
for me that I may be able to tell the boys at school.

R. T.

Though the spelling and the grammar were far from
perfect the sentiments were beautiful.

A GREAT VENTURE.

CHAPTER III.

AFTER twelve months' experience in work amongst the female prisoners of the County Jail, it was felt that little permanent good could be effected owing to the fact that when their term of imprisonment expired, did they desire to do better, the bar-room and house of vice stood wide open, while every respectable home and means of earning an honest livelihood were closed and barred against them.

Many in response to the oft repeated question, " Why do you not forsake such a life?" have said : "Where can we go?" " Who will take us into their homes without a recommendation?" "Where will we get our next meal?" Outcasts they were without a true friend or home, treated much as the lepers were in olden times, is it any wonder that many were found who would gladly avail themselves of any help that could be given them in reclaiming their characters?

The need was felt of a *Home* where a helping hand and shelter could be offered to any sinful, friendless woman without regard to creed, nationality, age or condition, at any time, night or day ; the only requisite being a desire to lead a better life.

A gentleman hearing of the need immediately offered the liberal sum of $400. towards the opening of such an institution, provided the young women who had been laboring to uplift their fallen sisters in the Jail would undertake the management.

After much prayer and waiting upon God to know His will, it was decided to accept the offer on condition that they should have the co-operation of an advisory committee of earnest Christian women.

No. 412 Wellington street was then rented, possession being granted in November, 1887, but owing to the fever epidemic, it was not opened till January.

Of these two long months of waiting, there is an unwritten history of evil prophecy, discouragement, and opposition. They were told that the respectable citizens of Ottawa would not support such a hot-bed of vice ; that they could not possibly manage such " vicious creatures as they desired to reach ; that it had been tried and proved that faith would not work in a city like Ottawa, and that they had better not adopt the " faith principle " for its support ; they were told also that it was a most un-popular work, and most unbecoming for *young* women to undertake. Hardly a day passed that letters of warning were not received asking them to take the fever as an evidence that it was not God's will that such a work should be undertaken.

On the morning before Christmas, however, upwards of fifteen members of the Bible class gathered in the newly-rented house, armed with pails, brushes, brooms, and other indispensable articles, known to the house-keeper, and together they whitewashed, scrubbed and cleaned the old building from attic to cellar. Yes, and furnished it with accommodation for fifteen inmates and a matron at a cost $247. Bureaus and wash-stands combined were made of inverted flour barrels with tops of white marble oil cloth and draped with cretonne, over which hung a small mirror. Evangelist Crossley, on the day of the opening, advised the inventor to get out a patent on it. Some are in existence to-day.

At nine o'clock Christmas eve, house cleaning being finished, a weary looking lot of girls met in the dining room, some with faces bespattered with white-wash, others showing traces of black lead, and just as they were they knelt and asked the Divine Friend of the friendless to come in and hallow each room with His manifested presence and love, and to make it a birth place of precious immortal souls.

Everything looked so clean and bright and cosy as they separated for their various homes. But while they slept "the sleep of the righteous " that night, a water pipe in the upper story burst, and all night long a torrent of water poured through ceilings, walls and floors. Imagine the picture of desolation which awaited them Christmas morning! To reach the supply tap in the cellar they had to wade through six inches of ice cold water and make their way through a beautiful cascade which dashed down the cellar steps, carrying with it bakepans, brushes, and other useful and ornamental articles. It was a scene never to be forgotten. The stoves which had been left so beautifully shining and bright were covered with white-wash, and ornamented with a fringe of icicles; the carpet in the reception room was completely submerged, and it too had its share of whitewash.

Surely, never did a work receive such a baptism of discouragement and opposition. It seemed as though all the forces of evil combined had arrayed themselves against them in order to hinder the commencement of a work which had for its chief aim the glory of God in the salvation of the most degraded.

On the 9th of January, however, the matron having arrived, the Home for Friendless Women was formerly opened with a dedicatory service in the dining hall. No sooner was the meeting over than the first inmate arrived—poor Zeph. St. Amand, a name well known in Police Court circles.

Over six hundred have since found a shelter beneath its roof. The following is taken from one of the annual reports :—

" As the faces of these ruined girls and women come " up before us our hearts yearn with unutterable pity for " them. Many were so young and being possessed of an " enviable share of beauty had been flattered and sought " for ; but alas ! upon how many a fair brow has been " written that pitiable word *unfortunate*. We can hardly " speak of this class without emotion. Often have we " wept and prayed with poor broken-hearted motherless " girls who have been more sinned against than sinful " Some on the very verge of despair have been almost " ready to take their own lives.

"It is from the ranks of these unfortunates that our
"abandoned women come. Often when the first fatal step
"has been taken and all hope of reclaiming their char-
"acter gone, they sink lower and lower until they lead a
"life of sin in order to support themselves.

"Miss Barber, of Montreal, in speaking of this class
"says :—*Abandoned girls*—abandoned truly, but by whom ?
"Abandoned, alas ! by Christian women, mothers and
"sisters who will one day stand looking into the tender
"eyes of Mary Magdalene's Saviour and tell Him why
"they left to perish those whom He came to seek and to
"save.   That they are not abandoned by God any one
"may prove who has faith and love enough to rescue
"them in His name,"

"We have seen more evidence of blessing resulting
"from work amongst these classes than any other.   The
"poor girls know they are lost and need no argument to
"prove that they are sinners and that their only hope is
"in Christ.

"It is a significant fact that during an experience of
"three years in this work we have not found one aban-
"doned woman who was not a victim of intemperance."

A large number of inmates were respectable women

and children who have been deserted by faithless husbands, a class which is increasing so alarmingly that steps should be taken at once to do something to remedy the evil.

Many interesting cases might be mentioned of those, who having sought shelter in their time of need, and having received impressions for good there, have turned from their evil ways. But space will not admit of a full statement of them. Three keepers of dens of iniquity who sought shelter in the Home to evade the police, have given up the old life and are struggling to earn an honest livelihood.

A poor orphan girl with no friends or home, said with her latest breath :—" Were it not for this Home I would have been eternally lost. Kiss me again ; no one has kissed me since my mother died."

Another, an English emigrant who had graduated in the school of crime at the early age of twelve, testified in a prayer meeting in one of the churches recently, that she had been picked up out of the gutter in a helpless state of intoxication, and brought to the police court on more than one occasion, but that she had been converted in the

Home and kept from yielding to the old temptations for upwards of two years.

In the Protestant Hospital is a poor girl whose life is fast ebbing away because of past dissipation. When the first symptoms of disease appeared she fled for refuge to the Home, and at the close of one of the gospel meetings was asked a pointed question about her soul's welfare. As she evidently did not wish anyone to mention the subject to her, she fled to her own room and securely fastened the door, but she could not shut out the question—it seemed to echo and re-echo in her ears—" How *shall* you escape if you neglect so great a salvation ? "

The Spirit of God soon worked deep and real conviction and she was led to cry for pardon and mercy ; for hours she seemed unable to get a sense of His forgiveness, until, on opening an old Bible, she read, " Neither do I condemn thee, go and sin no more."

Such testimonies, and these are not exceptional cases, serve to show something of the good that is being accomplished in the hearts and lives of the inmates, and not until the secrets of all hearts are revealed will it be fully known how many have been led to realize God's forgiving love.

Many were brought to the Home through three important ingathering agencies, viz :—Visitation at the Police Court ; the Prison Gate ; and dens of vice.

The Police Court of the present enlightened age, with its public sessions, is one of the grandest schools for the education of young criminals ever instituted. Here many are found who, having passed the entrance examination, are branded as belonging to the criminal class, and encourged in every possible way to begin a career of infamy and shame.

The following notes from the diary of one of the workers will speak for itself :—

Friday, Court crowded. Cabmen, shantymen, Lower Town saloon keepers, toughs of all descriptions, polluted the air with fumes of strong tobacco and whiskey, long before the Chief called " Order " and the Magistrate took the chair.

The first case called was that of a saloon-keeper. The charge—selling liquor without a license. Fine—$50 and costs.

Next, a young girl steps into the dock. She is tall, slight, fair and well-dressed. As the charge of larceny is laid against her, she is covered with shame and confusion.

The trial proceeds, rude, coarse jests are heard from the motley crowd in the rear. At length her whole story is before the court. She was a housemaid in a respectable family; had parents living in the country; was tempted to take what was not her own, and in an evil hour, yielded. "That is enough," said the Magistrate. "As it is your first offence, you may go, but if ever you are brought before me on a similar charge, your sentence will be a severe one."

Her face crimsoned as she turned and met the rude gaze of the crowd, and as she hurried down the aisle to the door, a rough fellow was heard to say to his companion :

"Come on Bill, she's a bouncin' fine-lookin' girl for sweet sixteen. Let's follow her and strike a mash." Before they could reach her, I had drawn her arm through mine, and led her out by another way.

"Where are you going?" I asked.

" I don't know," she replied ; " I've lost my situation. My month would have been up next week, and I have'nt a cent in my pocket. Oh, if I were only at home !" she sobbed, "this would not have happened."

"Would you like to go home ?"

"Yes."

"Then come with me, you can have dinner with us and we will see you safely to the train this afternoon."

A "pass" was obtained from the Mayor, and one more unfortunate rescued from the snares of evil men, and pointed to One mighty to save.

Saturday. The Smiths' case; which has been remanded for a week, came up this morning. Poor little fellows— one is only ten years of age ; the other, twelve. When I entered the court they were sobbing bitterly, and begged the Chief to allow me to sit with them inside the bar. The request was acceded to, and Tommy threw his arms about me and sobbed : "Dear Miss W——, do git me off jist this once, and I'll be a little Christian, so I will."

Their's was the last case called. "What am I to do with these little incorrigibles ?" said the Magistrate to the Chief, in an undertone. "This is the fourth time they have been brought before me in as many months."

"Their friend, sitting over there, has some plan on foot," said the Chief, "about sending them to an Industrial School, I think."

"Are you prepared to do anything for these boys ?" said the Magistrate.

" I have been in correspondence with the Superintendent of the Mimico Industrial School," I replied, "and he is willing to have them admitted, provided you will fill out these forms which I hold in my hand."

" And who is to pay for this benevolence ?" he asked. " The Industrial School Act provides that the municipality should be responsible."

" I fear," said he, "that the municipality of the City of Ottawa cannot afford to be benevolent to the extent of $4 per week.   No doubt, there are hundreds of mothers in the city like Mrs. Smith, who would be glad to avail themselves of an opportunity of pawning off their ill-brought-up sons on the municipality."

" But, sir, the municipality will spend hundreds of dollars in a few years in trying to reclaim them after they have become hardened criminals.   Would not the old adage : 'An ounce of prevention is worth a pound of cure,' hold good in this case?"   Nothing more was said, but, after giving them another severe reprimand, he dismissed the case.   As the little fellows bounded down the aisle, with a hop, skip and jump, fully a dozen street arabs who had watched the case with interest, gathered around them, while one said, excitedly :

"You're a brick, Jim!"

"It was your pluck that got you off," said another.

While one little urchin with a sling in his hand whispered: "Golly! but I felt like levelling my boomerang at the pate of that conceited 'bobby' that runned you in."

Monday found poor Mary Jones, *alias* Jenny Smith, *alias* a dozen other names, up again on the same old charge—"drunk and disorderly." Being unable to pay the fine, she was removed to the cells, where we found her giving vent to her passionate temper. However, all her efforts to smash and annihilate everything and everybody who came within reach, made little impression on the cement floor, solid stone walls, and iron bars of her narrow cell.

"Well, Annie," I said, "What is the matter?"

"What brings *you* here? you *heretic*, you *hypocrite*, you *hathen Chinee*. What are you prowlin' about this place for?"

"I heard you were in trouble again, and I thought I would drop in and see if I could help you. Turning to the constable, she said, 'Will you unlock this cell and let me in with Annie?'"

" Certainly, miss."

Soon we were locked in together, and, as the kind-hearted constable walked down the corridor, I seated my-self on the cold, hard floor, " her ladyship " occuping the only piece of furniture, a small wooden bench.

" Now, Annie, I want to have a little talk with you about——

" You can talk as much as you have a mind to ; 'twont do me any good," was the angry retort.

" Why did you leave the Home last week ?   You have been doing so well lately, and I thought you were trusting Jesus to keep you from yielding to the old temptation."

" He is not angry with you, dear girl, but it grieves Him to the heart to see you in this state."

" But look (handing her a pocket Bible) He says to you this morning, ' If you confess your sins He is faithful and just to forgive your sins and to cleanse you from all unrighteousness.'"

" There is no use talkin', Miss W———, He won't for-give me ; He has forgiven me so often already that I can-not expect him to do it again."

How many times have you asked Him to forgive you ?"

" Oh, hundreds of times ! "

" But, He says that we should forgive each other seventy times seven, or *four hundred and ninety times*. And do you not think that he is far more patient with us, and more ready to forgive, than we are to forgive each other ? "

" Do you think he would, *just this once ?*" she said. " It will be the last time, for if I yield again I'll give up tryin'."

We knelt together, and, as I took her hand in mine, it seemed cold and stiff. Never shall I forget the agony of soul through which the poor, weak, erring one passed. Her whole heart seemed to echo the language of the Apostle : '·Oh ! wretched man that I am ; who shall deliver me? until at length she had such a vision of Jesus as her only Saviour, that she could say : " Thanks be to God, which giveth us the victory through our Lord Jesus Christ." *

Thursday. Found Mrs. Nelson in one of the cells this morning, just recovering from a state of helpless intoxi-

---

* [It was the last opportunity I ever had of speaking to her. After serving her sentence she was admitted to the Home and, as she had evidently not recovered from the effects of excessive drinking, was confined to bed for a few days, where she was visited by the good Countess of Cavan, to whom she gave a beautiful testimony as to what Jesus had been to her in the past week. A few moments later she was found still and cold in death.

cation. She was in a sad plight, poor thing, having slept part of the night in a coal bin, and lost her shawl, hat and shoes, and was evidently much concerned about her children, whom she had left alone in a house on Albert street. As she was sent down for a month, we went in search of the neglected little ones, and found a beautiful curly-headed boy of five, asleep on the broad windowsill, his pale, wan cheek resting against the pane, while his little sister had crept into a clothes-basket on the floor which was half full of wet linen, and she too, was fast asleep. They had evidently been waiting and watching for mother until at length they had cried themselves to sleep. We took them to the Home, which was only a short distance away and where they were kept until their unworthy mother's release."

Many have thus been gathered in, among whom were a large number of young girls who were rescued from entering upon a criminal career, and sent home to parents and friends. Visitation at the prison gate at the hour when female prisoners are discharged, has been another means of getting some to seek shelter in the Home.

One cold January morning, an aged woman, clad in a thin calico dress, without a shawl, cloak or warm wrap of any kind, appeared at the gate. She was homeless and friendless, having been arrested the previous August for vagrancy, and so frail and feeble was she that it was with the greatest difficulty that she was led to the street cars, in which she was conveyed to the Home.

Comparatively few, however, come directly from the prison—some having homes of their own, others turning a deaf ear to the pleadings of those who seek their best interests, while quite a number are driven off in cabs before an opportunity is afforded of reaching them.

House to house visitation by the Bible woman has been another means of gathering in the lost ones. On more than one occasion she has visited houses of vice, and led to the Home a number of the inmates, who were too intoxicated to know where they were going. Four were thus rescued from a den in a narrow lane in lower town one evening, the mistress of the establishment having remained in the Home for two years, while one—a beautiful girl of sixteen, an orphan—was removed to the hospital, were she died a few days later from the effects of dissipation.

During the first eighteen months of its history, the work was carried on under great disadvantages, owing, partly, to insufficient accommodation, and to the fact that it was impossible to classify the inmates; so that those just entering upon a life of sin might be kept apart from those who had become hardened criminals. It was found, also, that laundry work, which had been started with a view to giving employment to the inmates, could not be carried on satisfactorily, as many of the women were physical wrecks, and unable for hard work; consequently, it was shirked and slighted whenever an opportunity presented itself.

In order to obviate these difficulties, it was decided to enlarge the building, and to purchase machinery for the laundry.

In March, 1890, the new building was ready for occupation, and great was the joy of the women as they moved from the dark, cold crowded wash-room, into the large, airy rooms where the work of the Home Steam Laundry is now carried on, and which is one of the best equipped laundries in the city. In the basement is a twelve-horse power engine and a large boiler. On the ground floor is an office, a sorting and wash-room, with a large hydraulic washer, a centrifugal wringer, starch dipper, starch kettle, soap boiler, and stationary tubs. Upstairs, in a large room 36x28 feet, and lighted by seven windows, are to be seen every day from fifteen to twenty-five women at mangles, skirt boards, shirt tables, starching tables, curtain stretchers, collar and cuff ironer, &c. ; and where there is also a dry closet and laundry stove, while on the third flat are seven bed rooms, with accommodation for eighteen persons. This, in addition to the old building, giving room for thirty-six.

The Home is not a place for the maintenance of the idle, as will be seen from the fact that hundreds of family washings pass through the laundry each month.

Nor is it, as some suppose, an institution for the encouragement of vice, the only cases ever refused admission being those unwilling to sign the following form of application :—

" Desirous of forsaking a life of sin, I apply for admission to the Home for Friendless Women, agreeing to the following conditions :—

" Not to leave the Home without the matron or assistant, until a situation or another home is obtained.

" To live quietly and peaceably with the inmates.

" To obey implicitly the orders of the matron."

Maternity cases are admitted solely on the following conditions :—That a paper drawn up by the magistrate be signed by all applicants in the presence of four witnesses, pledging themselves to remain in the Home for twelve months ; that each is required to care for her infant and to take it with her on being discharged, and that no case can be admitted a second time. The Board heartily disapproves of any arrangement or institution that provides for relieving the patients of the care of their offspring, thus rendering it easy for them to escape the full penalty of wrong doing.

When the young founders of the Institution decided to go forward in the name of the Master to open a door of hope to their less fortunate sisters, they believed that a prayer hearing prayer answering God could supply all their need without the aid of personal solicitation or the stimulus of bazaars, entertainments, raffles, &c., and they decided to look to Him alone for the support of the work. An experience of five years has proved that their confidence was not misplaced, God having honored their faith above what they had anticipated.

In taking a retrospect of His leading in the matter however, it would seem as though He has revealed to His servants the fact that "faith without works is dead," prayer having been answered through ways and means they never anticipated.

It was thought that the need would be met with the free will offerings of His people and thus it was for a time, but soon the laundry which had been opened to furnish the inmates with employment became a fruitful source of revenue and eventually the Master Himself placed the work on a self-sustaining basis, and with hearts filled with praise, they have learned to say with Miss Havergal. :—

He answered all my prayer, abundantly,
And crowned the work that to His feet I brought,
With blessing more than I had asked or thought,
A blessing undisguised and fair and free.
I stood amazed and, whispered, " Can it be
That he hath granted all the boon I sought,
How wonderful that He for me hath wrought !
How wonderful that He hath answered me."
O faithless heart ! He *said* that He would hear
And answer thy poor prayer, and He *hath* heard,
And proved his promise. Wherefore did'st thou fear,
Why marvel that the Lord *hath* kept His word?
More wonderful if He should fail to bless
Expectant faith and prayer with good success.

A MUCH NEEDED INSTITUTION.

CHAPTER IV.

IT has been said that " There are three words to whose music the heart never ceases to vibrate ; " *Mother*," " *Home*," and " *Heaven*." Specially is this the case with young women. Home and heaven are to many the sweetest words in human language because of their intimate connection with one who is to them the chief attraction—mother.

It is a lamentable fact, however, that there are hundreds of lonely hearts, in this city of mothers and homes, who have never realized the sweetness of either ; not that they are motherless, but *unmothered*, nor homeless but without the comforts and joys of a true home ; young women who crave that love and its demonstration, which is so lacking in many of the so-called *homes* of our working girls.

Anxiety and hard work seem at times almost to deaden natural affection in many parents, and cases have frequently been met with where girlish confidence has been repelled by those whom they call *mother*.

To them, home has no depth of sacred meaning, it is a mere boarding house which offers no brighter attractions than very ordinary table fare, and a bed with the children.

There are hundreds of others, sewing girls, shop girls, clerks, students, who, having left the parental roof to seek employment or educational advantages in the city, need a home and mothering. Think for a moment of the hardships, the loneliness, the need, of this class. Their limited means drives them to seek out the cheapest boarding house to be found, where a small, close, ill-ventilated room is taken and shared with two or three others to lessen expense. Hastily dressing in the morning they hurry to their uninviting breakfast. Unrefreshed they go out to their long day of toil or study. Evening finds them worn and weary, perhaps nervous and irritable as well. How shall they spend the evening? They have no good books, no pleasant and innocent recreation lies within their means. They are too weary to work, and they must have change. What wonder if many spend the free hours on the streets or in places of questionable amusement where undesirable acquaintances may be formed. Sunday comes and if no one invites them to church or Bible class they spend it idly lounging in their close little room, perhaps reading dime novels, or with such companions as can be found only in cheap boarding houses.

These and many other circumstances made it most desirable that self-supporting young women should have a *Home*, where love and sympathy would greet them, and where they could be mothered and shielded from temptation.

In order to meet this need as well as to secure a place of meeting for the Bible class, which had grown to have a membership of over one hundred, No. 98 Albert street, since known as the YOUNG WOMEN'S CHRISTIAN INSTITUTE was rented in January '89, the ground floor being fitted up as a class room and an office or study, the two upper flats with bed room accommodation for twenty.

Upwards of one hundred and fifty young women, mostly students and strangers have since found beneath its roof a bright, happy, Christian home, and friends, interested in their welfare. Scores of others have been assisted in obtaining employment, while hundreds without reference to social or denominational distinction have received sympathy, encouragement and help, and have found a hearty welcome in the classes and meetings.

During the first six months of its history, the attempt was made to establish classes in kitchen garden, cooking, dressmaking, art needlework, painting and vocal culture, with a view to bringing a large number of young women desirous of fitting themselves for spheres of usefulness in homes of their own under Christian influences. Experienced teachers were secured for the various classes and soon over two hundred names were registered on the roll books. So many applications were received for the cooking class, taught on the Huntingdon system, which limited the class to a membership of twelve, that it was necessary to form two other classes, one for servants, which was held in the evenings, one for young girls attending school, while twelve young women about to assume the responsibilities of housekeeping were enrolled in the third.

The attempt proved a success in every way but one. Boarders complained of noise from choral class, of irregularity of meals caused by the "cooks" having possession of the kitchen, while both teachers and scholars felt the need of larger accommodation, and as the Institute depended for its support upon the fees of boarders, it was thought desirable to discontinue all but the Bible classes until more suitable quarters could be obtained.

This work has been prosecuted without formal organization and without any appeal to the public, but a change in the method of operation has been made recently and the work established on broader lines. The Ottawa Young Woman's Christian Association has been organized the object of which is the assistance spiritual, mental, moral and physical of young women.

It is the purpose of its founders that it should be a grand agency in moulding and fashioning the character of the ideal woman depicted by Wordsworth in the well known lines :—

> "A spirit, yet a woman, too,
> " Her household motions light and free,
> " A creature not too bright or good
> " For human nature's daily food,
> " A perfect woman, nobly planned,
> " To warn, to comfort and command ;
> " And yet a spirit, still and bright,
> " With something of an angel light."

This object the association contemplates working out in the establishment of an ideal home with clean, well ventilated sleeping apartments and attractive dining room ready to provide every physical comfort ; with library, reading rooms, and class rooms, thus affording to many who would otherwise remain mere toil-worn machines, the opportunity of becoming thinking, reasoning, *social* beings ; with a bright large hall where Bible Classes, Gospel meetings and Prayer meetings can be held, and weary souls pointed to the rest that is so sweet to the toiler; with an employment office through the agency of which situations can be obtained ; with a well equipped gymnasium where students, sewing girls, and others with sedentary occupations can secure healthy exercise and physical regeneration, and with Committee rooms having facilities for carrying on such benevolent work as a Diet Dispensary, Flower Mission, Dorcas Club, &c.

Shall not the young women of our city who wield almost omnipotent influence in the home and in society have such an institution where facilities would be afforded them for the highest and fullest training of all their power for God ? Too long has the slavery of folly and fashion, the sleep of indifference, the death of wordly pleasure possessed many of our Ottawa girls. It is high time that they should awake to the realities of life and its solemn duties and sublime possibilities. The greatest need of this age is

Christian women, not *butterflies*. The young women of to-day will be the mothers of to-morrow and in promoting any scheme for their elevation we are not only labouring most effectually for the extention of the Kingdom of our blessed, loving Lord, but we are laying the foundations of bright, happy Christian homes.

LIGHT IN DARK PLACES.

CHAPTER V.

THE attention of the Christian world has been drawn recently to Gen. Booth's new book, "In Darkest England and the Way Out." In reading his awful presentation of life as it exists in the mother country, there arose in the mind of the writer a parallel in a modified form to be found at our very doors.

Did it ever occur to our readers that in our city with a population of 56,000 (including Hull) there are one hundred and forty licensed liquor stores and saloons from which the water of death flows day and night for the destruction of the people ; that hundreds of precious lives are being sacrificed upon the altars of Venus ; that upwards of 33,000 are worshipping at the shrine of "the Queen of Heaven and Mother of God."

Such facts as these led our little band of Christian workers to undertake an aggressive evangelistic work, and like many efforts of a similar nature it had a very small beginning.

While visiting from house to house in a narrow,

muddy lane leading off Chapel street, they found themselves suddenly and unexpectedly admitted into a low tenement in which were ten men, smoking, drinking and gambling. It would be difficult to imagine who felt the embarrassment of the situation most. Their first impulse was to withdraw as quickly as possible, with an apology for the intrusion ; on second consideration, however, they determined to look to the Master for protection, while they might tell as best they could, under the trying circumstances, the object of their visit, viz :—To warn lost men and women to flee from the wrath to come, and trust in Jesus for salvation. The surprise, the amazement in each face could hardly be depicted ; cards were dropped, tumblers and bottles moved aside, and a solemn hush came upon all as they spoke of the three " R's " Ruin, Redemption, Regeneration. After a few words of prayer, and the singing of a hymn, which by the way, attracted five other rough fellows from a neighboring den, they were invited to come again. As they did not covet another experience of the kind, it was proposed to rent a market hall in the vicinity for a meeting to be held once a week.

The proposition met with the approval of all present

and several signified their intention of not only attending themselves but of bringing their friends.

The following Wednesday evening the hall or loft having been secured at a reasonable rent, lanterns, borrowed mostly from the neighbors, were suspended from the beams, while seats were made of scantling laid upon blocks, a load of which had been deposited at the entrance of the hall, an old stove covered with rust and a three legged table being the only other articles of furniture. Snow drifted in from the broken windows which added considerably to the picturesqueness if not to the warmth of the first Mission Hall.

True to their promise came the crowd of roughs whose one aim in life seemed to be the finding of some new way of killing time. The first to arrive was a one-armed, one-legged gipsy pedler, who had just served a term in the Central Prison for horse stealing ; then came a low sized Frenchman known to the boys as John L. Sullivan. Upwards of twenty others, all men, had gathered by 8 o'clock, when the meeting commenced. They had evidently come for " a good time, " for when the attempt was made to sing the first hymn, several tried to drown the strains of music by shouting, " We won't go home till morning," while prayer was interrupted with loud hall-elujahs. They listened, however, to a short, pointed Gospel address, and after the last hymn was sung, dispersed very quietly.

The mission thus started is situated in the midst of the largest collection of snares set by evil men and women to entice into sin and ruin, in the city. Here it is that the lowest and worse elements of humanity are to be found, and that souls are swept along the downward way, night after night.

Intemperance is the chief sin, and it is undoubtedly the cause of nearly all the crime, vice and wretchedness, which the workers try in a measure to alleviate. In the midst of it all the mission stands as a beacon light to warn them of danger. The singing of gospel hymns from the balcony generally arrests the attention of passers by, and workers are engaged in urging all who come within its doors to abandon sin, seek the Saviour, and begin a new and better life.

The work has been full of interest and incident, though not as fruitful in results as one would wish. When we consider, however, the lives which many of these men and women have lived, nurtured and trained as they have been from earliest infancy in the school of ignorance and crime, is it any wonder that the work is a slow one? Good impressions received at the meetings are often dissipated because of influences of evil to which they are necessarily exposed. Many start out with a sincere desire to be kept from their besetting sins, but fall back again into their old ways. None but those who are constantly engaged in the work can realize how nobly and desperately many of these unfortunate victims of appetite and adverse circumstances struggle for the victory.

A fatherless, motherless boy, who lived with his sister in a home of shame, and who had become a confirmed drunkard at the early age of fourteen, staggered into the mission one night to hear the singing, was convicted of sin, and lingering with the inquirers at the close of the meeting, was easily led to decide to trust Jesus to save him from the power of sin. He became a regular attendant at the meetings for several weeks, but was found one evening at the open air service, evidently very unwilling to enter the hall. When asked the reason, he replied,

" T'aint no use, if a fellow had half a chance might be some hope for him. Last night when I went home found 'em all drunk, and I got mad, 'cause she (sister) called me bad names and I swore at her so I did."

"Oh Jack," said his friend, " did you not ask the dear Lord to forgive you and to save you from yielding to that old habit?"

" No, Miss."

" Why?"

" Cause," said he, almost defiantly, " I'm just waitin' to get her alone and, and——"

"You will tell her how sorry you are, wont you, my boy."

"Indeed I wont, I'll give her the biggest trouncin she ever got in her life, and you bet she'll never call me bad names again—might as well be killed for a sheep as a lamb—might as well wait till I've got a big sin to confess as a little one."

Will our readers come with us in their imagination to Jack's home. It is only a few steps from the hall. We enter a narrow lane or gateway leading off Clarence street and soon find ourselves in a muddy back yard, where stands an old out-building which was evidently meant for a stable or store house. As we enter there is not a trace of any-thing to show that it is inhabited by human beings. Heavy festoons of cobwebs are suspended from the ceilings, the few remaining unbroken panes in the windows are frosted with age, the door is ever open day and night and here the neighbour's chickens, dogs and cats find a refuge from the wind and storm. A rickety staircase leads to the second floor which is not much more inviting than the first. This upper chamber serves as parlor, dining-room, bed-room and kitchen, all in one. A pile of rags on the floor in one corner, with two salt sacks for a covering, serves as a bed for three. On the table are a number of unwashed tomato cans and sardine boxes, picked up out of heaps of refuse, which do good service as cups and plates. Here night after night drinking, dancing, card playing, are carried on until morning.

Is it not enough to make the angels weep to think of that poor orphan boy striving to lead a Christian life in the midst of such influences. May the Lord hasten the day when the Government shall see the necessity of establishing in Eastern Ontario an Industrial School similar to the one at Mimico, where youths entering a criminal career may be taken out of such surroundings and trained for spheres of usefulness.

Such revelations of misery, depravity and degradation

are not exceptional.   Illustrations are furnished daily of the power of strong drink to ruin, to degrade and brutalize both mind, body and soul.

A regular attendant at the mission is J. L.   He is a Frenchman of mature years though a dwarf in size.   His face reminds one of Dore's picture of the inhabitants of Dante's Inferno.   A better subject for a representative of Evil Incarnate could hardly be found.   Joseph, who is the only child of over indulgent but intemperate parents, learned to drink and smoke at the age of seven.   He never attended school and seldom went to Mass.   The profession he follows at present is that of night bar-tender in a Lower Town Saloon, his work lasting generally from 10 p.m. till 3 or 4 a.m., in payment for which he receives after each night's work a cheap bottle of whiskey.   This he carries home and shares with his aged parents.   Drinking is then indulged in until daylight when all three sink into a state of drunken stupor, from which they generally recover late in the afternoon or evening.   Joseph is then sober and ready for the evening meeting.   On one occasion the workers were under the painful necessity of having him removed from the hall for disturbing the meeting, and the following evening he took revenge by throwing into their eyes a handful of cayenne pepper. He was then lost sight of for several weeks. When told by a friend, however, that no action would be taken to have him prosecuted, he ventured to return one evening and manifested unusual interest in the meeting. On leaving the hall he was met by one of the young women, whom he had so cruelly treated, with a warm grasp of the hand and a few kind earnest words, that went right to his heart.

" Glad to see you back again Joseph, we have forgiven you and have prayed that the dear Lord Jesus may not only forgive but save you."

The Spirit of God seemed to work conviction for a time, but as yet no evidence has been given of a desire to forsake sin.

T. M. and J. S. are both fathers of large families Their children attend the mission Sunday School. They were once strong, fine-looking, manly fellows, but have long since lost good situtations as well as their manliness, their prospects, their health, their strength, their all, through strong drink. Both depend upon the meagre earnings of their overworked wives for support, and seize every opportunity of stealing from them the articles of clothing received into their homes to be laundried, that they may pawn them for liquor.

The men are not the only victims of intemperance in this locality. What a sad and terrible sight are the intemperate women! Some with little babes in their arms, who, as Bishop South truly said, are "not so much born into the world as damned into it," and who from the day of their birth, drink in the vile poison from their mother's breast. Is it any wonder that even the children are found with an insatiable thirst for it?

A poor little fellow, deformed and crippled, is a born slave of the bottle. His mother gives him all he wants whenever she can get it.

"Shure, it's his only comfort" she says, "the house is cold and food is scarce, and poor Charlie, it helps to keep him warm and comfortable-like."

Charlie's boy friends who make a few cents now and again, in disposing of rags, bones and bottles, put their little earnings together and spend it in liquor obtained from a grocer, who is told that it is for "ma," and together they have "A *spree* like grown up people."

Darker scenes than these are witnessed daily by those who have faith enough in the saving power of God, to go forth in His name to rescue them from sin and shame, for Bacchus is not the only false god who is licensed by the government and worshipped by our home heathen. What shall be said of the votaries of Venus ! Too long have public prejudice and perverted modesty silenced the church, the state, the press, from giving revelations which would shake society at the Capital to its very foundation.

The time for silence, for timidity, for false modesty for prudishness has long since passed, and those who hear the deep wail of anguish, and see the unutterable woe, which comes up from the abyss of moral corruption in our midst, are in duty bound to speak out.

We boast of our Sabbath-keeping, church-going people. We look with pride upon our thirty-two churches, and our numerous charitable institutions. We congratulate ourselves on the ever increasing amount given each year to foreign missions, while all the time young lives are being sacrificed in our very midst at the shrines of these false gods, as truly as in India where the heathen mother sacrifices her child to her idol.

Children have been found as young as fourteen with the awful realities and responsibilities of motherhood upon them.

Gay, giddy, thoughtless girls are being ensnared in dens of infamy and shame, which are not only tolerated but patronized by the law-makers of this guilty land, and by whom, alas ! they are being ruined as effectually and irrevocably "as one, who, for caprice might burn a priceless diamond into a chip of carbon, from which condition all the chemists in the world can never recover it."

That the deliberate author of a ruin such as this should be entrusted with the responsibility of a legislator—nay worse—should be permitted to come to the Lord's table and be received into the society of the good and the pure, is a sin and a shame.

Cases have been placed in the hands of lawyers who have expressed the hope that the grief stricken parents would "see the propriety of dropping the case, for if, brought into court it would involve the putting of good men into the witness box and he would be sorry to tarnish their reputation."

Do these men with greater advantages of education and position, expect when arraigned before Heaven's Court and Heaven's Righteous Judge, that He will acquit them, pronouncing them "good men," while he banishes the poor unfortunate to outer darkness?"

Scores of these dens are known to the police and in asking their co-operation in an effort to break them up, it has been found that however clear the evidence, neither magistrate nor police can interfere, unless parties living in the immediate neighborhood are willing to appear against them in court, and this they are generally unwilling to do.

From a human standpoint the work of the mission is a hopeless one. No amount of reasoning has any effect upon those who are so completely under the mastery of appetite and passion that they cannot break away from it, although they see the most terrible consequences staring them in the face : but the Master has bidden His servants " gather up the fragments " of ruined lives, the wrecks of hope and love, and bring them to Him whose very touch means healing and salvation. He alone can bring out of a lost manhood or womanhood, a new creation as many a living witness to His saving power can testify.

The most hopeful feature of the work in connection with the Mission, has been the Sunday School and the Boys' Brigade, in both of which the effort is made to go before and get the start of sin in the lives of the children by winning them for Christ.

On leaving the hall one evening, one of the workers overheard the following conversation between two children who had listened to the "old old story," evidently for the first time.

" D'ye hear what he sez 'bout a man with a *swear* name what died to save the likes o' us, do you think its true ?"

Shrugging her shoulders her little barefooted, bareheaded companion replied :

" Guess 'taint—its one of them stories what people reads in books."

It led to the formation of an interesting class of boys and girls, some of whom were black, some white, some were Gypsies, some French, all neglected little ones unreached by the churches. Quite a number have given evidence of true conversion and their prayers and testimonies are an inspiration to many older Christians.

" 'Tis sweet to watch the opening flower, but more
To view the budding beauties of a soul."

The Boy's Brigade was organized with a view to securing the attention and interest of a large number of French youths between the ages of fourteen and twenty, who were a constant source of annoyance and trouble in the meetings. They meet once a week during the winter months in the hall, when the following interesting programme is gone through with :

The singing of Gospel hymns to martial tunes, marching, calisthenic drill with dumb-bells and wands, concluding with a short Gospel address and prayer.

The Brigade is very popular amongst the boys, and as there is room for only a limited number, and as regular attendance and perfect order are made conditions of membership, an opportunity is afforded of giving the Gospel message in a well attended, orderly meeting.

Missions of a similar nature have been established at Cathcart Square and Hull under very trying circumstances. The Square is situated in the lower part of the city in what is known as Letter O District, which is densely populated by the working classes, and within a radius of a mile of which there is not one Evangelical church or Mission. Here, notwithstanding the bitterest opposition, the way of salvation by faith in a crucified Redeemer, has been preached to hundreds of French Roman Catholics, mostly boys and young men, every Friday evening. Four times the door has been torn off its hinges, windows smashed, curtains torn into shreds and benches overturned. Stones have frequently been hurled through the windows while meetings were in progress, but notwithstanding all, the work goes on, better order is being maintained at length and a deeper interest evinced in the work.

The stereopticon was found to be a grand agency in bringing the truths of the Gospel within the comprehension of this class. For instance, a hymn may be sung, such as "Jesus saves," as the last strains die away suddenly the lights are turned out, and a beautiful colored representation of the angel appearing to the shepherds brought out on the canvas, which affords an opportunity for a few earnest words on such passages of scripture as, " Unto us is born in the city of David a Saviour, which is Christ the Lord," or Mary's song, " My soul hath rejoiced in God *my Saviour*." Illustrations of the power of the Lord to save from sin may be furnished from scenes in the life of Peter.

A representation of Peter sinking, our Lord standing with outstretched arms ready to save him, illustrates the condition of the sinner, sinking beneath the waves of sin, powerless to save himself by any effort of his own, his only hope being in Jesus. A picture representin Peter's deliverance from prison, serves as a good illustration of how the Lord saves from the power and bondage of sin· The angel, which may be taken to represent the Saviour, finds Peter in darkness, asleep, bound, he lets the light shine in upon him, smites him to rouse' him up, strikes off the fetters,opens the prison and sets him free to serve. The idea can be developed or enlarged upon in such a way as to hold the attention and interest of the most incorrigible attendants at the mission, their reverence for such pictures going a great way in maintaining order even in a dark room.

On one occasion, after singing the well-known hymn,—

"Why not, why not come to Him now"

One of the workers spoke from the text, "Why tarriest thou?" mentioning among others the following reasons given by many for not coming to decision :

"I'm afraid I can't hold out." A picture of the Good Shepherd with the wandering lamb on his bosom illustrated the text, "Neither shall any pluck them out of mine hand."

"Too much to give up." The rich young ruler suddenly appeared on the scene and then Peter and John leaving all to follow Jesus, and it was pointed out that coming to

Christ does not mean giving up so much as receiving something infinitely better than the world could give.

"Too far gone, no hope for me now," says another. A representation of the Saviour at the tomb of Lazarus revealed His power to raise into newness of life even the most hopeless cases.

Another gives as an excuse, "I cannot see things as you do, religion is all an enigma, it doesn't appeal to my reason." Blind Bartimeus appeared on the canvas and it was shown that he could not see either, until he came to Jesus, and then he saw things as he never saw them before.

In this simple way deep and precious truths are brought within the comprehension of the most illiterate and the Master has set His seal of approval upon the work.

The effort to introduce into Hull the light of the glorious Gospel of our Lord Jesus Christ, must ever remain a memorable event in the minds of those who were called to the work.

What Isaiah said of the Gentile world may be truly said of Hull, "Behold darkness covers it and gross darkness its people." A darker state of things could hardly be found in "Greenland's icy mountains," or "India's coral strand," than exists at our own doors.

Let our readers picture to themselves a death-bed scene witnessed by two Christian workers, which is not an exceptional case, or in the least overdrawn as many can testify. A poor young French girl of about fifteen years of age was dying. Great was the sorrow in the house. The neighbors gathered in, amongst them several Protestants. As death approaches they fall on their knees and tell their beads a number of times. Every few moments the dying child is sprinkled profusely with holy water so as to quite wet the person who was holding her. Then a ball of some kind, supposed to have some mysterious power, was pressed to her sides. Every now and then a brass crucifix was placed to the young girl's lips and kissed, and when just about gasping the last breath, the brass image was put quite into her mouth and because her teeth closed on the image the friends were well pleased. Into the powerless hand of the poor dying child was placed a lighted candle. The hand being closed over it and held by a friend, and so with beads, balls, candles, crucifix and holy water in abundance the poor child passed away, and still the awful delusion does not end. Another young woman goes to the church and takes the wafer for the dead one.   The rest of the drama is being concluded by the priest, who is getting all the money he can from her poor relations and friends to pray her soul out of purgatory.   What a satire it is upon our Christianity and our civilization that the existence of such heathen darkness in our very midst should attract so little attention.   No doubt much of the indifference is due to the woeful amount of ignorance that prevails with reference to the teachings of the Roman Church.

Christian people have expressed surprise at the persistent efforts to evangelize the French, notwithstanding bitter opposition, and have said :—" Why not leave these people alone?   If they are true to their church and live up to the light that they have they will not be lost, for after all it doesn't matter much what they believe, if they are only in earnest."

The priests of Baal lived up to the light that they had and were terribly in earnest in crying to their false gods, but they fell under the just condemnation of the only true God.   Saul was true to his convictions when ' breathing out threatenings and slaughter against the disciples of the Lord," but who would say that it was pleasing to God. Salvation depends not upon *how* we believe but upon *what* we believe.

Of their earnestness and devotion there can be no question. They are a standing rebuke to many Protestants in this respect. But that they are LOST and under the condemnation of God is evident from the following facts :—

God says : "Thou shalt have no gods before me " (Ex. 20: 3); "Thou shalt worship the Lord thy God and Him *only* shalt thou serve" (Mark 4: 10), Roman Catholicism says : "Mary is the entire ground of our hope" (see Pope's letter to clergy 1832), while a devotional book in common use in our City and vicinity contains the following prayers to "the Mother of God."

" O Queen of the universe and most bountiful sovereign, thou art the advocate of sinners, the sure port of those who suffer shipwreck, the resource of the world, the ransom of captives, the solace of the weak, the comfort of the afflicted, the refuge and salvation of every creature. Hail thou who art the peace, the joy, the consolation of the whole world. Hail Paradise of delight, the sure asylum of all who are in danger, the source of grace, the *mediatrix between God and man.* Refuge of sinners pity us."

Again we read, " Mary is that celestial ark which will *surely save us* from wreck of eternal damnation if we on take refuge in time. The ark of Noah would only receive the few men and animals who were saved in it, but Mary receives and *saves with certainty* all who take refuge under her mantle. But, Oh ! my Queen, *how many men are lost ?* And why ? *Because they will not have recourse to thee."* If this is not worship. What is it ? It is an insult to God. It is ignoring the sacrificial, mediatorial work of Jesus the Son of God, of whom Peter said : " Neither is there salvation in any other, for there is none other name under heaven given among men whereby we must be saved," Acts 4. 12. And of whom Paul said : " There is one God and one mediator, between God and man, the man Christ Jesus," (1 Tim., 2. 15). The Lord evidently anticipated this apostasy in the Church when in Luke 11., 27, it is recorded that " a certain woman lifted up her voice and said unto Him, Blessed is the womb that bare thee, &c." But He said, " Yea *rather* blessed are they that hear the word of God and keep it," and this brings us to another evidence that these poor deluded people are lost, because the church falsifies and withholds from its people the word of God.

We read in Rev. 22 : 18. " If any man shall add unto these things, God shall add unto him the plagues that are written in this book and if any man shall take away from the words of the book of this prophecy, *God shall take way his part out of the book of life.*" We have only to refer to the Douay Bible to see the number of books that have been added and we may seek but in vain for the second command in the decalogue "Thou shalt not make unto thee any graven images." Rome has obliterated it and divided the tenth so as to retain the correct number.

Still another evidence of the lost condition of those who hold the doctrines of the Romish Church can be found in that they ignore the only true way of salvation, faith in the finished work of a crucified Redeemer, and trust to baptisms, masses, confessions, fastings, indulgences, good works and purgatory. "He came to save His people from their sins," was He not able to do what He came to do without the aid of all these things? Is it not most dishonoring to the Lord to doubt the efficacy of His atoning cleansing blood and to claim that " venial sins can be expiated only in purgatory ? "

The sight of a whole city bowing down to a false god, without the Word of Life, and without a knowledge of the way of salvation, stirred the hearts of several of God's children to undertake its evangelization. Accordingly a small house in one of the worst localities was rented and fitted up with seating accommodation for about fifty. Circulars were distributed through the streets inviting men and women to a gospel meeting to be conducted in French every Thursday evening. Long before the hour appointed a large crowd had gathered about the building which was densely packed as soon as the doors were open, those interested inwardly congratulating themselves upon the success of the effort. It was noticed, however, that the audience was made up exclusively of men, big rough fellows, who did not deign to remove either hats nor pipes when several lady workers entered. It was thought, however, that such uncouth behaviour was more from want of knowledge than lack of courtesy, and so they proceeded with the meeting though the air was stifling. After the singing of several Gospel hymns the French Colporteur addressed the meeting taking for his text, "For God so loved the world that he gave His only begotten Son that whosoever believeth on Him should not perish but have everlasting life." For nearly twenty minutes they listened attentively to a simple earnest Gospel address, when suddenly a piece of cord wood was hurled with great force at his head, missing it, it smashed to atoms a coal oil lamp. This was evidently the signal for an attack The workers were surrounded and dragged out into the street and kicked about the face and head. A policeman who appeared on the scene was powerless in such a crowd but dispatched messengers for help. Soon five others arrived who surrounded the little band and escorted them to the station under a perfect shower of stones, pieces of ice and sticks of hardwood. On arriving at the station, the police charged the mob which soon dispersed.

A possé of Ottawa police were then telephoned for, who conducted the little band to their homes in safety, and so ended the first attempt to evangelize the city of Hull.

The question naturally arose—what was to be done ? To abandon the field was to deal a paralysing blow, not only to French Evangelization, but to civil and religious liberty throughout the whole province, to maintain their rights as British subjects to hold a Protestant meeting in a Roman Catholic community, meant evidently the sacrifice of precious lives. It was a question which perplexed some of the best minds both in the church and state, for great fears were entertained for a time of open rebellion and civil war. While the question was under consideration in the House of Commons and in almost every pulpit in the city, God was testing his servants and bringing them to the point of willingness to lay down their lives if need be that Hull might have the glorious light of the Gospel. It was then decided that a meeting should be held as advertised the following Tuesday evening. Almost immediately an offer was received of an escort of one thousand armed men. It was declined however, as it was felt that it would be more in keeping with the mind and will of the Master, that everything should be avoided that had any tendency to stir up strife. So it was arranged that two young women who had taken a prominent part on the previous occasion should go alone, protected only by Him who said, "Fear thou not ; for I am with thee, be not dismayed for I am thy God, I will strengthen thee, yea I will help thee ; yea, I will uphold thee with the right hand of my righteousness."

The promises never seemed so sweet and precious as when they crossed the bridge and found the whole city in a state of excitement. Groups of men were to be seen on almost every street corner, talking excitedly in French, while now and then could be heard such threats as "We'll drive the 'Suisse' (a term first applied to French Protestants converted through Madame Feller, a Swiss lady, who established a mission near Montreal) into the river." "We will blow up the hall." "If they come over to-night they will be carried back," &c.

As they turned into the dark, narrow street that led to the Mission Hall, they were met by a fine, stalwart specimen of Christian manhood, who said :—

"There is going to be serious trouble to-night, a mob of several thousand surrounds the Hall. What will you do?"

"God has sent us," was the reply, "He will protect us or be responsible for the consequences."

"You will go, then?"

"Yes."

"Then I will go with you."

For a moment they hesitated, arguments were used to try and make him break his resolve for the sake of his wife and seven little ones who were dependent upon him, but he too had learned to trust Jesus and if ever his faith was called into exercise it must have been then. Some difficulty was experienced in gaining access to the Hall owing to the great crowd which had assembled. The chief of police was on hand, however, and cleared the way so as to enable the workers to enter.

As soon as it was ascertained that "the Suisse' had arrived a revolver was discharged which threw the whole crowd into a state of confusion and uproar. The Chief of Police and his little band of men tried to quiet the mob promising that meetings of a similar nature would never again be held in Hull, but it was of no avail, fire arms were freely discharged, the building bombarded with stones, windows and doors smashed and it seemed for a time as though hell were let loose. The meeting was held notwithstanding, and if ever there was earnest pleading with God for the lost in the City of Hull, there was then. It lasted for fully one hour when suddenly there was a lull, the loud oaths and curses seemed to fade away, there was a cessation in the stone throwing, (many having gone to the quarry for a fresh supply of rocks, as it was ascertained afterwards,) and it was feared by those in the building, who, by the way, were all Protestants, that the whispered threats with reference to the blowing up of the building was about to be accomplished. It was noticed that the neighbors had removed and this confirmed their suspicions which proved afterwards to be groundless. Quick as thought the lights were turned out and the door quietly opened, and as heavy shutters covered the windows of the room in which the meeting was held, it was not noticed by the crowd that one after another had filed out into the darkness and made their way quietly through the mob to the Police Station where a horse and sleigh was waiting to convey them safely to the other side of the river. Thus God fulfilled His promise in protecting those whom He led out to establish the Mission, though many who had bravely stood up in their defence were seriously injured. So ended the second attempt to introduce the Gospel into Hull.

The third was made the following week and cost the city council $500.00 for special constables. Perfect order was maintained however and their right to carry on an an undenominational evangelistic mission vindicated.

It was necessary to secure better and safer quarters for the work, the old Hall having been left in a shaking con - dition, and as a suitable place could not be rented, a building on the same street was purchased in which meetings have been held ever since. House to house visitation has been carried on with some measure of success, and copies of the Word of God have been placed in a number of homes. The following notes from the diary of their French Missionary show something of the good work that is being carried on :—

What can be more touching than to find street after street, closely packed with small houses filled with people hungering for the Bread of Life. We called this afternoon at a certain house and asked if they would like to possess a copy of the Bible. They had never heard of such a book and we explained that it was about the life of Jesus. Men, women and children gathered around as we read the old, old story, and the unanimous opinion was that "it must be a good book," and they were easily in-duced to purchase a copy.

An old man of over seventy lived in the next house and as we read to him the story of Nicodemus he stopped in the midst of filling his pipe, with tobacco in one hand and knife in the other, and seemed so eager to catch every word. We left him a copy on approbation (one of De Sacy's translation, having on the title page letters of endorsement from Cardinal de Noailles, L'Abbe Courcier and several other prominent men in the Roman Catholic church), and on calling the following week found that it had been burnt by order of the priest."

Surely such facts as these should stimulate all true believers in the Lord Jesus to more earnest, self-denying efforts for these unsaved ones in our midst. Never before "since the day when Our Lord's hands were nailed apart to embrace the whole world, has there been a greater need of heroism like that of Paul or Stephen.

On every side surrounded by the light of the Gospel are thousands who have never heard the joyful news of salvation by faith in the finished work of Christ. Who then will help on this blessed work either by placing themselves at the disposal of the Holy Spirit to be fitted for an obedient, devoted and aggressive line of welfare against sin and error or by contributing to the support of the work. Too long has the Church ignored the last wish and command of her Lord, "Go thou into all the world and preach the Gospel."

Too long has the pleading cry of Jesus, "Whom shall I send and who will go for us?" been met with the reply "Here am I send *him*." God wants your money or your life for this work. Shall he not have it?

One month after the opening of the Hull Mission, March 3rd, 1890, the Ottawa Gospel Mission Union was organized with a view to uniting under a Board of Management, the missions referred to and establishing such other agencies as might be used of God for redeeming the bodies and souls of those who seemingly cared little for either.

Like the Young Men's Christian Asssociation and the British and Foreign Bible Society the Union is strictly evangelical and unsectarian, its membership consisting of men and women in good standing with the various evangelical churches who were deeply impressed by the necessity of more united aggressive efforts to spread the knowledge of the Gospel among the unevangelized thousands in our midst. It was felt that such work could only be done advantageously through co-operation on the part of Christians of all denominations. For obvious reasons no one church could do it effectually. The number of workers available would not be sufficient, and even if this were not so the fact of its being undertaken by a denomination would narrow the sphere of its operation.

The work of the Union includes the missions at Anglesea and Cathcart Squares and Hull ; house to house visitation by Bible women, the publication and distribution of tracts having a local reference, special evangelistic meetings in halls and churches, parlour Bible readings, cottage meetings, training classes for Christian workers, and last but not least the Gospel waggon.

A large pleasure van is rented twice a week and filled with twenty-five or thirty earnest workers who take with them an organ, a cornet occasionally and a good supply of tracts and papers. Driving out to districts destitute of churches and missions they begin to sing bright, stirring gospel hymns with now and then a solo. Soon a crowd gathers and an interesting congregation it generally proves to be. Here stands a man in his shirt sleeves enjoying a quiet smoke, there is a woman in rags with a tiny baby in her arms, just opposite is a bar crowded with men who come out to hear the singing, even the bartender with his long white apron stands at the door and for a time drinks in the pure clear air of heaven without the poisonous fumes of whiskey and tobacco. Quite near is a dancing hall where twenty or thirty couple are tripping the light fantastic, they rush to the windows and doors, regardless of the orders of the dancing master. Soon the whole space is covered with people willing to listen to the gospel. Scores of men are there who would not attend a place of worship if they could ; poor, over-worked mothers are there who couldn't if they would, while way back in the darkness are ladies and gentlemen who happen to be passing and would like to listen without being seen, for the Nicodemuses are not all dead yet. Only those engaged in the work can fully realize what a privilege it is, to look into the sad, unsatisfied faces of these dear ones and speak to them of Jesus. All that Ottawa wants is more of *Jesus* and less of creeds and forms and ceremonies and what the Gospel Waggon seeks to do is to point the multitude to " the Lamb of God, which taketh away the sin of the world."

While the meetings are being held tract distributers leave the van and mingle with the crowd when opportunities are afforded for personal dealing with souls. A young worker approaches a rough fellow, and offers him a tract, at first he refuses to accept it, and then calling to her, he says.

" Say miss, I'll take it and read it too, if you believe in purgatory."

" I do believe in purgatory," is the ready reply.' " Purgatory means to purge, to cleanse, to purify, the blood of Jesus Christ is my purgatory, for it has cleansed me from all sin." Another is met with a request to visit a dying mother, who is unsaved, while another receives a warm shake of the hand and an earnest " God bless you, take this toward the expenses of the work."

Four meetings are generally held each evening during the summer months and thousands who would not be seen going into a church or mission in daylight, creep around under cover of darkness, pretending to be indifferent and listen to the singing and preaching of the truth.

It is a recognized fact that the largest proportion of our city congregations are women ; and if men are to be reached the place to do it is out on the street. What right have we to say that the Gospel shall be preached in the churches or missions only and then say to the people if you do not come and get the Gospel where we put it, you may die in your sins ? Shall we not do as Jesus did, go to them and offer them the Gospel where they are ?

Down through the ages comes the call, like a clarion peal from the trumpet of the great Captain of our Salvation, " GO OUT QUICKLY INTO THE LANES AND STREETS OF THE CITY AND BRING IN HITHER THE POOR AND THE MAIMED AND THE BLIND." " Who then is willing to consecrate his service this day unto the Lord ? "

RETROSPECTION ·
AND ANTICIPATION,

CHAPTER VI.

ISAIAH was once permitted to have a little glimpse of the glories of heaven and in his graphic description of the ministering spirits about the Throne, said : " Each one had six wings, with twain he covered his face, with twain he covered his feet and with twain he did fly."

In looking back over these seven years of service for the Master with its failures and discouragements, its lost opportunities, its disappointments one feels like hiding the face like the seraphim from the praise and congratulations of man and veiling the feet of all past services with the wings of higher aspiration and flying away to "regions beyond" to higher and harder things for God.

"They turned not as they went ; they went every one straight forward."

"*Forward.*" Shall it be so ?

This is a matter that each individual reader has a share in deciding. There are fields white to the harvest yet unoccupied for want of men and means. There are lost ones waiting and longing for deliverance from the power of sin. What has been accomplished is as nothing compared with what is yet undone. Never before was there such a need of *direct effort to save souls.* Time is short. Jesus is coming and He is calling to His own to consecrate their time, their means, their social influence, their opportunities their all to this blessed work.

Young Women, will you not help "forward" in building up a Christian Association, the sacred influence of which will be felt in all ranks of society not only in this city but throughout the length and breadth of the Dominion?

Mothers, as you look into the pure sweet faces of your own dear sons and daughters will you not help to carry forward the glad message of salvation "into the darkest and saddest dens of sin and sorrow in this city and bring some mother's boy or girl out to breathe the sweet fresh air of holiness and let the sunlight of heaven fall upon their pale, sweet faces and gladden their crushed and blighted lives? Forward! Until in an ever increasing multitude of hearts and homes our King is "loved, honored and obeyed."

Fathers, brothers, will you not help forward in maintaining a perpetual evangelistic society in the Mission Union. Churches are engrossed in their Sunday schools, their Young People's Societies, their prayer meetings and other agencies for the edification of their members, all of which are so necessary ; but who will help to reach out after the churchless ? Who will help to bring Christ to a Christless Christianity ?

The need is felt not only for workers, but means with which to build " three tabernacles," one without delay for the Young Women's Christian Association ; one before 1896 for friendless women ; and one before 1898 for the work of the Mission Union, with a large auditorium where evangelistic meetings would be held every night and discharged male prisoners and " out of works " furnished with cheap board and lodging and with temporary employment in an adjoining wood yard or broom factory.

The Master is bidding His servants " go straight forward." He is offering them grand opportunities of expressing their love and devotion to Him in the sacrifice of their time and means, and He will not fail to reward them.

We read that in the dark days when the returned captives were slowly struggling to rebuild Jerusalem, a few friends came from Babylon bringing treasures of gold to aid their brethren in the erection of the temple. The gifts were received and a beautiful memorial was prepared, the gold moulded into crowns, bearing the names of the givers and placed on the head of the high priest and then hung up in the Temple of the Lord in remembrance of their sacrifice of love. Beautiful type of the honor God will give to those who give Him gladly of their means. It grows into crowns in the heavenly Temple, which Jesus is not ashamed to wear as an everlasting memorial.

"A little while," for winning souls to Jesus,
  Ere yet we see His beauty face to face ;
A little while for healing soul diseases,
  By telling others of a Saviour's grace.

"A little while" to tell the story,
  Of Him who made our guilt and curse His own,
"A little while" ere we behold the glory,
  To gain fresh jewels for our heavenly crown.

'Tis but a little while, the way is dreary,
  The night is dark, but we are nearing land ;
Oh ! for the rest of heaven, for we are weary,
  And long to mingle with the deathless band.

—F. R. H.

SUBSCRIBE FOR

The Friend ≡

——OF THE——

≡ Friendless

AN INDEPENDENT MONTHLY JOURNAL
EDITED BY THE AUTHOR
AND

Devoted to the dissemination of the Gospel, the culture of the Christian life, and to aggressive evangelistic and rescue work.

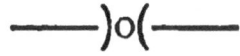

TERMS:—Five cents per copy; fifty cents per year.

TRY
The Home Steam Laundry.

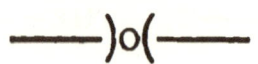

TERMS :—House linen and ordinary articles of underwear, 30 cents per dozen. Starched clothes extra.   Lace curtains a specialty.

Parcels called for and delivered to any part of the city.

Further information may be obtained by telephone, or from the matron.

HOME FOR FRIENDLESS WOMEN,
412 Wellington Street.

THE FOLLOWING

TRACTS Having a local reference and suitable for distribution among the unsaved, can be obtained at the office of the

FRIEND OF THE FRIENDLESS

No. 98 ALBERT STREET,

OTTAWA.

——)o(——

THE PRODIGAL SON AND HIS IMITATORS—

By C. F.—5 cents per dozen or 35 cents per 100.

FAILED—By B. H. W.,—5 cents per dozen or 35 cents per 100.

THE BEE AND THE BONNET—By B. H. W.— 5 cents per dozen or 35 cents per 100.

www.ingramcontent.com/pod-product-compliance
Lightning Source LLC
Chambersburg PA
CBHW020809020726
47495CB00008B/2646